I0402605

Cash Pad

Build a real estate empire in less than 30 days
with no money, no experience, and no credit!

Ryan Hansen

CashPadBook.com

Acknowledgements

A big thank you goes out to my mom for instilling the belief in me at a young age that anything is possible. Without you, I wouldn't have the confidence to go after my dreams. You are the best mom a son could ask for and I love you.

To Stacia for accompanying me to every coffee shop while I wrote this, cheering me on to keep going, and being my first editor. I love you so much.

And to all the guests who inspired me to write this: you all rock and it's been a pleasure having you in my home every weekend!

Cover art by: Jimmy @ MascotAgency.com

Editor: Eric Wyman

Formatted by: Brian Kananrd

Contents

Part III: Hosting

Preface

This is a book about real estate, but not in the traditional sense. I'm not an investor, agent, or flipper. I own a small gym and my background is actually in fitness. I couldn't tell you a thing about "walk scores" or "CAP rates", but I can teach you how to squat. And although I went to college and consider myself to be a relatively smart guy, the real estate biz has always intimidated me. Just the words *mortgages, contracts*, and *banks* make my blood rise. But despite feeling overwhelmed, I was still interested in learning about the ins and outs of real estate, but I didn't know where or how to start.

With never enough cash for a down payment and no investor willing to let a guy with zero experience take risks with their money, the barrier to entry was a mile high. So over the years I read books, watched YouTube videos, and dreamt about it. But I never had the stomach or the means to play the market. You can make enough for retirement or lose your entire savings just by a single deal. No industry before has ever created, or destroyed, such wealth.

That was, until I discovered Airbnb and the new sharing economy...

This book is broken up into three parts: Starting, Building, and Hosting.

The first section, Starting, is my origin story. It's about my first Airbnb experience and how I bought a loft and started a side business.

The second section, Building, is where I discuss the business of short-term property management. Where to find spaces, how to find owners, and how it all works.

And finally, the third section, is Hosting. I'll share how to set up your space and how to give your guests the best possible experience.

I purposely choose to keep this book short and sweet, choosing brevity over fluff. You should be able to finish it in a few hours, giving you plenty of time to go out there and take action.

This is my first book, inspired by the fun I've had being a host, the money I've made along the way, and the questions I get asked about. I hope you enjoy it!

Part I: Starting

Chapter 1:
<u>Chicago</u>

My first experience with Airbnb was back in 2015. My girlfriend at the time and I drove up to Chicago for an obstacle course race, one of those crazy things athletically inclined people do where you roll around in the mud and climb through barbed wire. Sounds fun, right? Rather than get a hotel like a normal person, I thought it would be cool and more affordable to stay in someone's apartment via this new "home-sharing" website I had heard so much about. Luckily, my girlfriend was the adventurous type and on board.

I still remember how nervous we were calling the hosts upon our arrival. We were about to walk into a lived-in apartment and sleep on a stranger's bed! What did we agree to? But as it turned out, our anxieties were immediately dismissed when the welcoming couple greeted us in the lobby like old friends; it all turned out better than expected.

It was an experience I'll never forget.

My girlfriend and I had the best time that weekend. The race kicked our asses, we stuffed our faces with deep dish pizza at a local joint, and we took the train every chance we could get. We felt like true Chicagoans, living in the big city. We weren't in a hotel district and the concierge didn't push us into tourist traps. It was different and we loved it. Sure, the bed was slightly uncomfortable, sirens blared by during the night, but we didn't care. We were living like locals; an authentic first-hand experience in the heart of the Windy City.

We loved staying in strangers' homes!

Interested in how it all worked, we learned our hosts bought a place just outside the city and instead of selling their apartment, they chose to rent it out to guests, primarily on the weekends, as they retreated to the suburbs for some peace and quiet. Chicago was busy enough, so they had no problems filling it up. Given the $120 per night rate we paid, I estimated they would pocket about $1,000 a month. With Airbnb, they were paying off the mortgage, possibly living for free, and gaining equity in their home. I thought that was a pretty good deal.

Those few days in Chicago changed everything for me. Now, after staying at dozens of Airbnbs over the years, I can say they were some of best hosts I've ever encountered, and because of that genuine first impression it's probably why I got hooked and am such an advocate for it after all these years. Had we been left outside waiting to get checked in or if the place was a mess, I wouldn't be where I am today. So a big thanks goes out to the nice couple in Chicago for setting me on a journey I never expected.

Over the next couple of years, I was an Airbnb fanatic, staying at dozens of homes across the country. The spaces were all unique; farmhouses, treehouses, and surfer shacks, all offering something far more special (and cheaper) than you could experience from staying at a hotel.

Then I had coffee with a friend, who in passing conversation told me she was renting two apartments downtown, listing them on Airbnb, and pocketing $2-3k a month. (This is now called rental arbitrage. Where you take advantage of pricing inefficiencies in the market and buy low to sell high.) Needless to say, I was taken aback. I'd always assumed you had to own the property to do that and it never occurred to me you could rent and then sublease.

The wheels started turning. With this approach, the opportunities were boundless. Every apartment, house, or loft was fair game and all you needed was a signed lease. You didn't need a mortgage, a down payment, or even an investor. This was my way into real estate.

Now mind you, I'm a dreamer and an entrepreneur. As a kid, I put on magic shows for my family and even sold tickets. As a teen, I downloaded music from NAPSTER and made bootleg mixtapes to sell in the schoolyard. As a grown adult, I opened up a gym and started a fitness brand.

That coffee meeting with my friend was one of those fateful moments where it snapped for me. I knew Airbnb and short-term rentals were going to be huge. It's like feeling the subtle vibrations of an earthquake and if you're reading right now, in 2019, you're feeling it too.

With the lease on my apartment ending, it was the perfect time to make my first move into real estate. I took a different approach than my coffee friend did and decided to buy.

To me, buying a home is a liability, not an investment. But in this case, I could now make my home an asset through renting. And better yet, with Airbnb it was all easier than ever before. I could become a landlord in a few short hours by setting up the extra bedroom, snapping a few pictures on my phone, and posting it online.

For months, I searched and searched until one Sunday morning I got lucky and found a beautiful 3-bedroom loft the day it got listed. It was perfect; cool, hip, and very Airbnb. I called the agent and left a message. He called back within the hour and told me they had an open house the day before and already received two offers. I was bummed and about to hang up when he said I could try to put an offer on it anyway.

Not knowing a thing about home buying (I told you I don't know much about this) I thought an "offer" meant it was a done deal. He explained that sometimes things fall through, like the buyer doesn't have the financing, they can't get approved for a mortgage, or they change their mind. Relieved, I rescheduled all my clients the next day, a Monday, and went to tour the space.

I had to keep my tongue inside my mouth once I walked in. It was even better than the pictures. I snatched it up with the full intention of renting out the extra bedrooms and away I went, taking my very first steps into short-term rentals.

I moved in on April 15, just two days after my 30th birthday. I couldn't think of a better present to myself. And what a day that was. Years and years of 12-hour days as a personal trainer, client after client after client, and here I was, standing in my dream pad.

Before this, I had a small one-bedroom apartment and moved in with a hand-me-down couch and a scruffy IKEA bed frame to my name. After I was settled in, I started buying furniture and after about three months of hardcore thrifting, I was ready to set up my listing.

I talked to another friend who was managing Airbnbs for a family she worked for. Wet met up and had my loft listed within two hours. It was far easier setting up than I anticipated. A few days later, I had my first booking, a group of women from Ohio in town for a bachelorette party. Coincidently, I had an out-of-town tattoo appointment the weekend they were staying so they had the entire loft to themselves, which made it easier since I didn't know how to act with strangers in my house yet. My friend met them at the unit for the check in, key exchange, and grand tour, and I kept it touch with them through the messenger app. It went off without a hitch.

With the space being so unique and a five-star review to kick off my newfound career as a landlord, I got more bookings that week. Soon enough, every weekend for the next month was full.

I was hosting people from all over the world, from New York to Switzerland. From a tuba player trying out for the St. Louis Sympathy to an Olympic gold medalist. Over time, I got more comfortable with staying with strangers, it covered my entire $2,000 mortgage, and, as an added bonus, it forced me to keep my house clean.

Things were rockin'! Running my gym was fun, but this was something entirely different. It required less of my time, I had happy guests that sometimes brought me their dinner leftovers, and I was hanging with good people every weekend.

Chapter 2:
<u>Scaling Up</u>

I told everyone who would listen about my positive experiences as a host. After a year of having guests in my spare bedroom, I was training a client when she mentioned that a real estate agent on her Facebook feed was asking about Airbnb. I had experience and knew enough about it, so I sent her a message. It turns out she was trying to help a client list their condo. The owners were a retired couple living in Arizona for six months out of the year during the harsh Missouri winter (if you've ever been to Missouri, you know exactly what I mean). Now they wanted to host while they were away.

The messages went something like this:

Me: Hi Joan, I saw you were looking to help a client manage an Airbnb. I have one myself downtown and would be happy to help.

Joan: Sure, what management company are you with?

Me: I manage them myself. It's pretty simple. Do you mind passing along the client's information?

I then immediately called the owner and causally explained how I've been a host for a year and loved it. I offered to help set his account up and manage it if he'd like. He seemed interested and told me he would talk with his wife.

I sent a follow-up text a few hours later with a link to my listing, so he could see the reviews and the professionalism in which I hosted. We set up a meeting later that week.

Lesson: Act quick. Follow up, follow up, follow up!

The night before, I put together a proposal in Microsoft Word. I found a picture of his apartment complex on Google, I typed in the zip code on Airbnb to find comparables, and listed my duties and costs. I presented it and they agreed, happy to cover their mortgage instead of paying for the place to sit empty, like they had done in the past.

For a copy of what I designed and presented to them, go to CashPadBook.com/proposal .Whatever you decide, make sure you print using thick cardstock. I used Kinkos.

I now had my second listing and duplicated the same process I used to set up my own. Professional pictures, a well-thought-out description, and a house manual. I hired a cleaner, I googled "remote locking system for Airbnb", and I went live when everything was in order.

This space was different than my loft, which guests booked as an experience. For the condo, guests wanted utility (I'll explain the difference later in the book). The place was a small but well kept and clean 2-bedroom, 2-bath condo 20 minutes from the city, in a suburb of St. Louis. I priced it to compete with a hotel room, figuring that a family with kids could book it as economical alternative.

It worked. We had our first booking within a week. It didn't fill as fast as the loft though, most likely because of the offbeat location, but it still covered the mortgage for them, even after my management fee.

Here I was, making a few hundred bucks managing another listing that only took a couple hours of my time. I'd answer messages, send a text to the cleaner after a booking, and I made sure everything was running smoothly. I had improved my methods and systems from my time hosting in the loft so the guests were satisfied, regularly leaving 5-star reviews. I was helping a couple pay their bills while making extra money. With the smart lock we installed, I didn't have to meet the guests. It was pretty much a hands-off business.

I had, by accident, created a short-term property management company. An official sounding business that might require an office, a front desk, and staff with check-lists and meetings to attend, but I was a solo operator, running it all from my phone in-between clients at the gym. It was a lean, profitable, and simple operation with no overhead or extra expenses. So, it didn't take long before I got it in my head to find more.

Lesson; if it works for you and another person, it will work for others.

There is a historic section of St. Louis with 100 beautiful, magazine-worthy homes. Back in the 40s and 50s, STL was the bustling gateway to the west, ahead of Chicago. Big money built some of the most incredible homes you could ever see. Big white columns, stained-glass windows, and fountains in the front yard. I loved that area and thought guests would love staying in a house with history and character. They'd feel like royalty.

My client, a real estate agent, helped me get the names and addresses of the entire neighborhood. I took out paper, drew up a flyer, but then scrapped it in favor of a letter instead. This way it would stand out, be more personal, and hopefully not tossed out with the junk mail.

I typed up a rough draft in my phone notes, I edited it, I got second opinions, then I edited it some more. After about a week, I had a friendly but professional letter. Succinct and direct, with every word having a purpose; I didn't want to waste anyone's time. I had seconds to grab their attention, so I had to make this a letter worth reading as well as an offer worth considering. I positioned it as an opportunity for extra income without any work on their part. I'd take care of everything and direct deposit the payout into their account. In a neighborhood of means, an extra $1,000 a month wouldn't make a difference but people like money, especially when it doesn't involve any work. It was a long shot with my hope being these were second homes and not lived in much or that they had been on the open market for 6+ months and hadn't sold. Or perhaps they had a second home somewhere else that they could list. There were lots of possibilities and it could go any which way.

At the last minute, my client suggested I hand write the letters since she had success doing it with her business. Ugh, I thought, what a hassle. But she was right, it would show that I took the time and care, so maybe they'd give me a shot. I went to Target, bought blank quarter-sheet note cards with envelopes, and got to work. I wrote letters every chance I could for the next week and a half; while waiting for clients, before eating dinner, even in traffic. I had to get them done as quickly as possible because if I lost momentum and delayed, I'd quit. I knew I would get discouraged if I didn't hear a response. So everyday, I'd write 10 letters, no matter what, which would take me an hour. This habit was a trick I learned from Jerry Sienfield and Steven King, who wrote daily, even on holidays, and it seemed to work out pretty well for them. After I finished, I'd handwrite the address, put on the stamp, and send it off.

A few days after I sent them all, I got four calls. One wasn't interested, but was impressed by the effort, as he was in real estate himself. Another had considered it for a while and would get back to me when she returned from London. Another wanted to buy a building, convert it into short-term rentals, and needed someone to manage it. And someone else had a house they'd be trying to sell in the suburbs for a year without any success.

Lesson: You never know. A single "yes" could change everything. Don't assume "No" until the other person says it themselves.

The house for sale was the most promising and immediate. She left a message and I enthusiastically called back within the hour. I had confidence in my voice knowing that my little side business worked, after now having two properties running smoothy. I kept the conversation casual and brief, explaining how I was living mortgage fee and was helping another couple do the same. She too had a goal of covering the mortgage until the house sold. So we set up a meeting, I put together the proposal the night before, and we got together at the end of the week.

We hit it off, she agreed to the terms and we set a launch date for November 1st. I offered to help move some of the furniture and stuff out since they have been living in between homes. I used the real estate pictures for the sale in combination with some I snapped on my phone.

I downloaded a free property management contract, signed and sent it, and we were good to go. We had our first booking within a week, a 3-night stay totaling $580. And we had another a week later for $995, then another after that for $919. Over the first couple weeks, I collected $758 in management fees minus $300 for cleaning expenses. I netted $458.

That month I had a total of $3,300 in bookings, then $6,500 the next! I made more money than owning my gym, it required less of my time, and everyone was happy; guests, owners, myself, and Airbnb.

I was still living mortgage free, the couple in Arizona had their mortgage paid off while they were away, and the couple trying to the sell their home now only had one mortgage to cover instead of two. Sitting in a coffee shop looking over the numbers and thinking about how simple this all was, I decided I was going to share my experience. *Anyone can do this*, I thought. It was the easiest business to set up and there are millions of people in the same situations I encountered. People with second homes that sit empty, retirees that move between homes, houses that sit for sale as the market softens, guesthouses and mother-in-law suites that are filled with boxes and junk. The vacation and short-term rental industry is nothing new, but now it's wide open. Anyone with a computer and a phone could get in.

This is just the tip of the iceberg, since Airbnb is still a baby. Be glad you picked this book up when you did because as I write this, in 2019, the world is changing so fast, Airbnb included. And this exact opportunity, the way it stands right now, won't be around much longer. I predict the next two years to be the "Gold Rush" era for short-term property management through Airbnb; the time the industry talked about for years to come when they share their "remember when..." stories.

This looks a lot like the 2000s dot com craziness or 2015's social media buzz. So congratulations, you just walked into an opportunity that could change your life! Now let's take a look behind the curtain and see how you can make this happen.

Chapter 3:
Why Home Sharing?

As we become more connected virtually, we lose connection to the real world. Despite all the technological advances, the expanded social network, and all that's available at our fingertips, there is and always will be a deep-seated human need to establish relationships with those around us. Now more than ever do we need to feel connected to each other.

Uber, WeWork, and now Airbnb are examples of the new peer-to-peer, or sharing, economy, which I believe sprouted from this need. This is just the start, as these billion-dollar companies didn't exist ten years ago and aren't going away anytime soon.

Moving past the human element, home sharing makes sense for everyone involved. For guests, it's typically a more affordable option than a hotel. Most nightly rates are below that of a hotel and with a full service kitchen, guests can prepare their own meals, thus saving even more. This makes traveling more accessible and more attractive to more people. The whole travel industry has been broken up thanks to companies like Airbnb.

Also, staying in someone's home is a unique experience every time. We know the host likes Shel Silverstein and imported olive oil, all without never actually having met them. For a hotel, a Marriot in Dayton looks like one in Albuquerque. They are sterile and standardized, and today we want a more individual, authentic experience.

Finally, many of these Airbnbs are tucked away in a hidden neighborhood that would otherwise never be known. This makes for an adventurous and interesting trip. It's pulling people to explore new areas, spreading the economy in its wake.

For hosts, you can pay off the mortgage, most people's biggest expense and source of stress. Normal hosts average $1,000 renting out a spare bedroom. If you're the social type, you can meet people from every corner of the world and make friends. The stories, insights, and perspectives are a priceless education in people and the world. Hosts regularly use the platform as guests themselves and house swap. You could host a couple from Italy and have a place to stay on your next vacation. And my personal favorite, you become an ambassador to your city, giving recommendations and guiding your guests to have the best time possible. You create a real, local experience that guests are appreciative of.

And for you, the manager, it's a feel-good, easy business with a lot of opportunity. Beyond the initial setup time, it runs itself. Keep in touch with the cleaner, have a maintenance guy in your back pocket in case of an emergency, and be accessible via your phone for questions. You can run this completely location independent. But it's not all sunshine and rainbows. Like any business, I've had problems. One time a guest shot a rap video and set off smoke bombs, another clogged the toilet so bad we had to pull it out of the ground. Luckily, I have a good team and both my cleaner and the maintenance guys took care of it while I was across the country.

Home-sharing has been a godsend. I've always wanted to be in real estate (and you probably do too, since you picked up this book) and now anyone can. I'd feel the deep dread of FOMO after hearing stories about flipping homes and selling them for a $100,000 profit or an investor that sat on a rundown neighborhood for a few years and made millions. Despite wanting in, it was over my head. The lengthy contracts, the loan contingencies, interest rates, and the risk would overwhelm me and I'd give up. Until now…

With short-term property management, you don't own anything. Which means no down payment, no mortgage, and no risk. You don't have to worry if the market crashes, if you would lose your job, or for some unforeseen reason Airbnb went bust. You can, at any time, walk away from all this and move on.

Keep in mind Airbnb is a combination of two of the biggest industries ever; real estate and technology. It's leveraging technology, using a streamlined platform with millions of users with hard assets, like land and property. To top it off, it's wrapped up in travel, leisure, and escapism. Things we always value and want. It's big. Period.

Chapter 4:
<u>No Experience Required</u>

My 14-year-old cousin could do this.

I used Airbnb for years as a guest before jumping to the other side of the fence as a host, not knowing a thing about hospitality. But after a year of hosting guests every weekend and listening to feedback and reading reviews, I began to understand what it meant to actually be a great host. During my initial year as a newbie, I learned firsthand how to prepare a space, meet guests' expectations, handle a grievance, and interact.

But starting out, I was ignorant and didn't know what I was doing, but that's a good thing. It allowed me to do things that I now look back on and think *how did I pull that off?* As I sit and write this, I'm surprised that it's working out the way it is. Keep in mind, I have no experience in real estate, property management, or hospitality and I'm running a profitable short-term management business. Sometimes being too dumb not to know any better is a gift.

I'm telling you my story in hopes to outline a simple and straightforward approach to a mini real estate empire. With this, you will save the wasted months and money I spent when just starting out. When short-term rentals first peaked my interest, I bought books much like yourself. But the authors made it seem difficult. When I was ready to list my loft, I enlisted the help of my friend, and she walked me through the setup in a couple hours. It was all so easy, far simpler than I had imagined. After a couple clicks, a few uploads, and some typing, I was an active host booking stays and making money. I had a business!

It's okay not to have a Pintrest-worthy listing. You don't need a Temperpedic mattress or 500-count Egyptian sheets. (All things I thought had to be the best. It wasn't until I started getting consistent 5-star reviews that I realized most things I wanted were nice to have but not necessary.) Provide a clean, tidy, cool space and everyone is happy. And since home sharing is so new, guests are more forgiving and understanding. Most realize they aren't staying at the Four Seasons and thankfully, many privately share feedback of improvements like better towels, a fan in the bedroom, not enough plates.

Put on blinders; don't listen to those who say people are going to tear up your couch or steal your TV. Yes, those things could happen, but you could also get in a car crash. Does that stop you from driving? Ninety-nine percent of bookings are without problem.

Make it up as you go, keep it simple. Shoot for 3-5 listings and you can manage it all by yourself. This is the only business I know of that requires minimal time, no money, no licenses, and no overhead. It's crazy more people aren't doing this.

Chapter 5:
Perks

Off the top of my head, unless it's one of those MLM scams, I can't think of any other business you can start in 30 days that requires no money and no experience. It sounds too good to be true, but I know hosts making $100,000 a year managing just a handful of listings. This is a new spin on an old business, with plenty of opportunity.

For the purpose of this book, I'm only outlining a small management company you can run by yourself or with a friend or partner. I'm not talking big teams, 50+ listings, and a lot of moving parts. With my model, I believe you could make an extra $1,000 to $5,000 a month as a side business just by managing a few listings. That's almost an extra $50,000 a year!

This is a simple and easy business that doesn't require a lot of your time. At the end of the day, provide a clean space, make sure the guests have a great experience, and you'll do very well.

I love Airbnb as a guest and now I love it as host. I love reading reviews from the couples who had an amazing time exploring the city or the families who got together for Christmas. It's an incredible and fulfilling experience in a lot of ways.

Short-term property management through Airbnb will bring you more money, more free time, and more control of your life.

Part II:
<u>Building</u>

Chapter 6:
Location, Location, Location

This might surprise you, but according to Forbes the top cities for margins (booking rates/cost of living) are Charleston, Indianapolis, and Cleveland. Some of the lowest margins are Seattle, LA, and Denver.

The two paths for short-term management are targeting popular travel destinations, which seem like the most common sense approach, or shifting to less common places. I prefer the latter and I'll explain why.

You might be tempted to jump into a hot market because of never-ending demand. I know a property manager in NYC that has a 95% occupancy rate while in St. Louis. I average about 60%. But with high demand comes competition and there are currently 50,000 other, mostly look-a-like Airbnbs in the city for guests to choose from. Then there's laws and legislation. The hotel industry isn't fond of hosts sliding in their lane and siphoning off their guests. The stakes are high and hotels are willing to fight and they have the money, lawyers, and politicians to do just that. Paris, Germany, Santa Monica, and Barcelona have already completely banned Airbnb, making it either illegal or highly regulated. If you're in a major city, don't worry. You can still get away with it as of right now. The NYC property manager I mentioned is profiting $50,000 a month with 30 listings. That volume is out of the scope of this book, but there is opportunity everywhere. Contact all potential clients in major cities because they may have second homes or know of someone who interested. You just never know.

Second-tier cities are the hidden gems of a successful Airbnb business. For one, Airbnb was created for the people. Mike and Sarah from Kentucky couldn't afford the $300 average rate of a hotel in a major city and they didn't want to stay in a Best Western, but now they can head to New Orleans and stay in a Creole cottage a block off Canal Street for $100 with a host who knows the area. That's a huge shift in culture, traveling, and human behavior and it will drive Airbnb and your business straight to the top. Small towns and cities will keep your business booming.

Geographically, any listing in close vicinity to a city center, public transport, or a high-demand area (Eiffel Tower, a ballpark, a national park) is a hot spot.

Airdna.com is a research tool that shows the data for any city. You can see demand, daily rates, occupancy, percentage of growth, and the number of active hosts. In a few minutes you can get an overview of an entire market and learn the characteristics of the most successful listings.

A high regulation score = low regulation

A high demand score = high travel demand

A high seasonality score = the change between seasons is low

Chapter 7:
Experiential, Economical, and Extra Large

There are three types of short-term rentals.

The first type is experiential spaces. The most popular site-wide listing is an airstream on top of a mountain in California with a ridiculous view of the valley below. The second is a treehouse in an Atlanta backyard without a bathroom and air conditioning. Both spaces are different in setting, but offer an experience like none other. With that, they are highly successful, with a 6+ month waiting list and a $500+ nightly rate.

Airbnb was created by art students who appreciate design. Odd spaces like houseboats, glass domes, and farms have fueled its growth, beating out other vacation rental sites that seem stale in comparison. Unique and experiential spaces are the reason I sent letters to the grand manors of St. Louis. Who wouldn't want to feel like royalty for a few days?

Cool homes with good curb appeal and design will always be popular, as Airbnb and guests love them the same. They tell a story, help us escape, and light up our emotions. Think Disneyland. These spaces are diamonds, as they're harder to find but always valuable.

The second type is economical space. Most listings will fall into this category. The condo in the county serves its purpose as a less expensive option than a standard hotel. For $90 a night, you get a clean two-bedroom/two-bath place with a full kitchen. Like my first Airbnb in Chicago, a nice studio apartment close to public transport is a big hit.

Guests that choose this option are spontaneous, budget-conscious, mid-20s and 30s guests who want a weekend getaway with a place to crash. They'll be out and about exploring, checking out an art museum, or going to the donut shop they found on Instagram.

The third type is extra-large spaces with 4+ bedrooms designed to accommodate families, parties, and events. The demand may be less, but the nightly rate is high. Typically, the more people you host, the more you earn. Since it's often split between guests, you can charge anywhere from $300-$1,500 a night. Know a farmer with a converted barn? A divorcee with a midcentury six-bedroom estate? Those are hitting both experiential and extra-large for a double win.

No matter what you manage, whether it's a studio apartment in Boise or a beach house in Malibu, make it stand out. I once heard a guest say in disgust how so many Airbnbs are "chock full of cheap Ikea furniture." Scroll through the listings of any city and you'll see exactly what she's talking about; a lot of neutral, generic homes without any real character or pop. Theme your space. We named the loft the Coolest Loft in the City and filled it with graffiti, a motorcycle, and a projector screen with a massive couch.

I'd recommend diversifying your business, much like any smart investment portfolio, so you hit every traveler market; those that want something cheap and easy, fun and exciting, or big and accommodating. Hit all the buckets.

Chapter 8:
<u>Locating Owners</u>

Most of your time will be spent here, finding someone willing enough to give you their front door key.

It's all a numbers game. Contact enough people and you'll find your golden goose. My mother sold insurance door to door in Brooklyn in the 90s and told me if you tie a policy to a dog in Time Square and let it run, eventually someone will sign it. There are millions and millions of homes up for grabs to manage; you just have to find them.

The first is family and friends. Who do you know that travels often, has a second home, or too many bedrooms? Approach them and just ask. "Hey, let's rent out your place. I'll manage it. Here's how much you can make and what I can do to help."

The second is befriending a local real estate agent. Help them first. Do you own a coffee shop, a landscaping business, or a hair salon? Whatever you do, give to them first in order to establish a genuine relationship. Tell them your plan and see if they have clients or investors who would be good candidates.

The third is Zillow. A house sitting on the market is a money pit and you could offset an owner paying two mortgages like I did. Target homes on the market for 6+ months. Let them know you can block out dates for showings or only book guests during the week, since most occur on the weekends. Also, try Craigslist. Search "lease breaks", "subleases", and "moving". Airbnb got its start by building a bot that sent emails to anyone who posted, asking them if they wanted to list on Airbnb as well.

The fourth is landlords. This may take more convincing, since landlords tend to be risk adverse, but I know hosts who are doing this and doing very, very well. You take on risk, because if the listing doesn't book like you had hoped, you have to cover the loses. However, the solution would be to find an open-minded landlord and cut them in on a percentage instead of signing a lease.

The fifth is bandit signs. I haven't done this personally, but I would if I exhausted my other resources. These are the signs you every day stapled to telephone poles or stuck in the grass at a stoplight that say "We buy Homes in Cash". Some are handwritten, others are printed. They work, otherwise you wouldn't see them. So how about putting "Live rent free? Let's talk Airbnb! Call or text me @ XXX-XXX-XXX."

My preference is working with individuals who have vacation homes that sit empty or those with a house on the market for 6+ months. I find people are happy to get their mortgage covered.

Chapter 9: <u>Negotiating</u>

Most people barely use their vacation homes more than once a year. They sit empty and cost money. If you show an owner how they can now get their home for "free" by paying off their mortgage every month through short-term rentals, you'll become their best friend.

If the owner is already renting their home and you can show they can earn more, getting above the market rate without any time or effort on their part, it's a no brainer.

Here's how to handle a lead:

- Initial conversation (Call! Don't text or send a message)

- Set up a meeting within 2-3 days at the property

- Put together proposal printed on good paper (Kinkos)

- Show up on time and well dressed

- Walk the space with them, then sit down and go through proposal

- Set a firm date to launch
- Send them a management contract (Free from Google)

Selling points:

- They pay off their mortgage and gain equity
- Extra money for a vacation or home renovations
- It requires absolutely no work on their part; all you need is a key and use of the space
- Airbnb's $1 million insurance policy
- You can try it for 6 months and shut it down if not what they expected

Remember: You have an advantage in that most people aren't familiar with Airbnb and, like I was once, may be interested but mistakenly believe it to be difficult to set up a listing and manage guests. My clients are older, as most homeowners are, and new technology is slowly adopted so this is the time to act.

Your goal, job, and top objective is to make renting as easy and painless as possible, without any time or added effort on their part. This is why they pay you as the manager. Keep the checks coming and take care of any problems you encounter - upset guest, broken toilet - on your own.

Chapter 10:
<u>Networking</u>

Other hosts are a great resource and are often time happy to help. If you find a listing you're inspired by or curious about how they got started, don't be shy and message them. Be upfront, real, and honest. After, all people love to talk about themselves.

I found my cleaner through a host I messaged directly. While looking to book a space in NYC for a friend going to a convention, I noticed multiple listings had the same young, 20-something woman as the host. After clicking her profile, I was surprised to see she had 12 other apartments throughout city. I knew there had to be more to the story, so I asked her and she gave me her contact information.

"She" actually turned out to be a "he". It was a guy managing listings under female aliases, which he found to be the more bookable gender. We talked for 30 minutes, sharing tips and tricks.

There are Facebook groups for both local Airbnb and short-term rentals that you can be a part of. Turn the notifications off because FB groups tend to be very active and the alerts will drive you crazy. Become a part of the community, ask questions, and share your experience.

If you're the outgoing, social type, <u>Meetup.com</u> is another great resource. Find short-term rental groups that have weekly meetups and happy hours.

Connect with other hosts in whichever way you feel most comfortable and they will more than likely show you the ladder to the top. Copy other successful hosts and learn from both the good and bad. Success always leaves clues.

Chapter 11:
Launch in 30 Days

As a general rule, you should condense the time you estimate for anything in life by half. I wrote this entire book in two weeks, a task many would think takes months, maybe even a year. You can be up and running and booking guests within 30 days.

A week and a half to find a listing

The week after to set up a meeting, draw up a proposal, and come to an agreement

The week after for pictures, write descriptions, and find a cleaner

The week after to work out any kinks and do a run through.

Bing bam boom! Speed is the secret weapon in this business and those that act quickly are handsomely rewarded.

Part III: Hosting

Chapter 12:
What's in a Listing

You have a quarter of a second to catch a potential guest's attention as they scroll through the listings. The first way to do just that is by having a great picture. The second is your title.

Great pictures sell. Back in 2009, when Airbnb first started, the company wasn't getting the traction they hoped for. They realized hosts took amateur pictures that made their spaces look dumpy and unattractive, so the company sent photographers around the country to do it themselves and the rest is history. Remember, art and design drive Airbnb more than any other vacation rental site. People browsing expect to see aesthetically pleasing spaces, and that starts with great pictures. I'd recommend hiring a vacation rental or a still life photographer. Airbnb also has photography services they can recommend and even pay for, if they deem it worthwhile.

Great pictures:

- Show your space in the best possible light, literally. Shoot in the daytime with the lights on and the blinds open using a panoramic shot to show off every corner of the room, covering all the angles.

- Highlight the details and extras of the space, like the original, restored staircase or the ultra-plush towels. Do you have a bike guests can use? Show it.
- Have a cohesive theme, style, and flow.

When organizing your photos, use 3-5 pictures for each room, showing the different aspects starting with the best photo first. Put them all together. There needs to be a sequence, as if you were walking the space. Have all bedroom pictures, than all living room, and than outdoor.

Bad pictures:

- Are shot in portrait mode
- Shot in direct sunlight creating shadows and shade
- Are messy, blurry, and too dark
- Are mismatched and jumbled. Shot at different times of day, different quality
- No flow or continuity.

A standard real estate photographer may work, but that could be pricey and make your listing look like an ad. I think you'd be better off using a more creative spin. Think more Architectural Digest rather than HomeBuyer.

As a resource, HomeJab.com is an on-demand photography service that is reasonable with a 24-hour turnaround.

Beyond photos of your space, include five photos of the surrounding neighborhood and your favorite spot, as well as attach screenshots of your top two reviews.

Captions matter, too. Avoid short, factual statements. Instead of "patio", say "Enjoy a glass of wine while overlooking the city. On a clear day you can see the arch!"

The second thing a guest will notice, after the pictures, is the title. Using the same principle of a caption, create the experience and emotion.

For example, phrases like "*Luxurious Barn with New England Barn*" and "*Malibu Dream Airstream*" are better than "Convenient three-Bedroom" and "Cozy Renovated Studio".

Example: Adjective + Property Type + Landmark

Cozy 1 BR studio Near Time Square - 2 min. walk

(Good for economical listings)

Example: Adjective + Property Type + Feature

Modern Farmhouse with Lakeview

(Good for experiential)

Example: Adjective + Property Type + "Perfect for"

Luxury Estate Perfect for Large Groups and Parties

(Good for extra large listings)

For the body of the listing, write somewhat casually. Be concise and include some of your personality. Write about the details that make it your own. Maybe you have the most comfortable couch in the world or a porch that's great for people watching.

Chapter 13:
Host Profile

Trust is at the top of the funnel when it comes to bookings. A guest must feel safe, secure, and comfortable. It's a risk, especially for first timers, to jump into a stranger's bed. One of the biggest pushbacks from early Airbnb investors was the potential for staying with a psychopath, but to my knowledge that hasn't happened and people are actually good.

A good way to build trust is through reviews, as mentioned in the previous chapter. Another way is through the host profile, where you can show you're a normal, friendly, and safe human being like all the rest.

Once a guest is interested and clicks on your listing, they are brought to a page with more information and one of the first things they see is you, the person behind it all, with your picture and name.

A picture is worth a thousand words, so showing a smiling, clear, and friendly shot is best. The guest has the option to find out more by reading a short bio about you. Take the time to describe yourself in an upbeat and positive tone; who you are, what you do and enjoy, etc. What do you like most about hosting? Did you grow up in a big city, but now live in the country? Is your favorite food fried chicken? Guests want to know who they're staying with.

As an added layer of security, verify yourself and earn a green check by uploading your ID or passport to Airbnb.

All of above will relieve any tension and make the guest feel like they're staying with someone they already kind of know. That, in addition to answering messages in a friendly manner, will help close the gap between stranger and friend.

Chapter 14:
Outsourcing

I spend only an hour a week running the business, because I outsource pretty much every task.

For cleaning, I use Care.com, which I found via another host, and among cleaners you can also hire babysitters, dog walkers, and assistants if you'd like.

Post a job seeking weekly availability and hourly pay. Most charge a flat rate so they can rush a job, but keep looking for a $15-25 hourly rate, letting them know they'll have multiple, consistent weekly jobs.

Interview five, pick one, and have a back up. A good cleaner is crucial and the most important part of the business. Your listing must be spotless or a guest will ding you and knock you down in the ranking. Find a reliable, trustworthy, and professional person and do whatever you can to keep them, because I've had multiples over the year and most flake out on me, do spotty work, or are just plain unreliable.

Pay them well, explain that guest turnover is more detailed than a standard residential cleaning, and appreciate the work they do. A thank-you text or a gift every so often goes a long way.

To find your cleaning fee for a listing, do a test run to see the time it takes. If your cleaner is $20 an hour and it takes 2 hours, price slightly above. Most cleaning fees range from $25-$200 depending on the size of the house. For an extra bedroom in a loft, it's $25 and for a massive 4-bedroom manor its $150.

Give your cleaner this checklist to use as a guideline.

Bathroom:

- Completely wipe down shower, toilet, and mirror
- Vacuum to remove all hair
- Stock toilet paper
- Stock and roll towels
- Refill soap dispensers
- Living room:
- Fluff cushions
- Lint roll furniture
- Vacuum and sweep
- Kitchen:
- Wipe countertops
- Empty trash
- Empty and wipe out fridge
- Wipe down stove
- Clean microwave
- Clean coffee maker and restock

Bedroom:

- Hotel-standard bed made
- Fluffed pillows
- Vacuum and sweep; especially corners
- Check under bed for dust or lost items
- A dim, soft light left on if possible

Think of walking into a hotel room… better yet, a hospital. It's immaculate. You could eat off the floor. Now copy that. Every listing needs to feel clean and smell fresh. No Hilton would have soap scum in the shower, hair on the floor, or dust under the bed.

For maintenance, go to TaskRabbit.com and find a "general handyman" with great reviews. I found a guy for my loft after I moved in for odds and ends, like a broken toilet and installing a light fixture, and he's who I call if I have a problem with my listings. I've only had to do it once when a guest clogged a toilet and it was leaking, but it's always a good idea to have a reliable and affordable option you can call in a pinch.

For messages, use SuperHostTools.com to automate the most common ones. I've signed up for 14-day trials with other Airbnb automated messengers and they have too many bells and whistles that would take weeks to learn. I love SuperHostTools because it's cheap, easy, and exactly what I need. For $5 per listing, per month, you can set up a sequence of messages to guests and alert the cleaner after every confirmed booking.

Beyond the automatic messages, I personally answer all other inquiries, usually about pets, children, parking, early check in, and I communicate with the guest directly during their stay if needed. To run your management business on 100% autopilot, hire a personal assistant using ZenDesk.com or VirtualStaffFinder. com and once you answer a question, make it a template and have them do it in the same way.

Here's the sequence of messages that are automatically sent:

An hour after booking:

Hello Zach

Thanks for your booking! We're excited to host you. Will this be your first time in St. Louis? Please let us know if there's anything we can do to make this trip better. Have a nice day and we'll see you soon.

- Ryan

The day before check-in:

Hi there, do you know what time you'll be arriving tomorrow? You are welcome to check in anytime after 3PM and full instructions are within the app. If you have any issues locating or entering the home, please call or text me right away at 914-557-9812. Travel safe!

After their first night:

Good morning, Zach. Just checking in. How was your sleep? Was the temperature okay? Let us know if there's anything we can do to make your stay more enjoyable. There's coffee on us in your welcome basket, or for a full breakfast head on over to Rooster's on Grand Blvd. It's only a five-minute drive and they serve delicious omelettes. Enjoy!

The night before check-out:

Hey Zach,

Thanks for staying with us, it was our pleasure! Please make sure all the lights are off and just leave the key on the desk. We'll take care of the rest. We'd also greatly appreciate a quick review. If your stay was anything less than 5 stars please let us know privately so we can address it. Feel free to grab some snacks for the road on your way out. Check-out time is 11AM. Sleep well and come back and see us again :)

A week later if they haven't left a review:

Hey Zach, just a friendly reminder to please take a minute and write us a review. They're important to maintaining my Superhost status, so I'd really appreciate it. Thanks again and have a great night!

Chapter 15:
<u>Design</u>

I designed my entire loft by scrolling through Pinterest at night after work. I'd get ideas - like a magnetic strip in the kitchen for knives or mix-and-match styles like a living room with whiskey barrels - and create a board to refer back to.

Ideally, you can find a space furnished or staged. If not, as an added service, you can design it yourself, if you are artistically inclined, or just hire a designer.

Sources from lowest to highest:

- Goodwill and Salvation Army: Changes daily. Great for cutlery and plates, trinkets, even furniture.

- Craigslist: Know what you're looking for and search regularly. You'd be surprised. I got 120-pound whiskey barrels from a local guy who delivered them, which saved me on shipping.

- Ebay: The worldwide Salvation Army.

- Etsy: Unique, one-of-a-kind pieces. Artisan and handmade, so somewhat expensive. My chandelier is whiskey rings handmade by a couple in Tennessee and guests always comment on it.

- Wayfair: Regular coupons make this a solid, reliable source for pretty much anything. A one-stop shop with a ton of vendors and options.

- CB2: Crate and Barrel's more moderately priced sister company with a classic twist. Can get pricey, but it's quality stuff if you have the cash.

- Article: Clean, modern Scandinavian goods. Think of it as a more stylish and durable Ikea.

- Google: The mega source for everything else.

Make it home-y. Get personalized and incorporate elements that are uniquely you. Put touches of your own personal flair into it - whether it's objects you've collected or things that reflect your hobbies and interests. I once saw a listing that had touches of elephants to reflect the host's love of India and his travels there. Store any expensive items, antiques, personal clothing, and toiletries away, but leave out a few things you want to share.

For great examples of spaces I find to be interesting and designed well, head over to CashPadBook.com/design

5 design tips:

1. Use a focal point in the living room like a painting, accent wall, fireplace, or unique piece of furniture.

2. Have a theme. Could be modern, industrial, classic, hippie. When possible, use local artists and the environment for inspiration. Keep in line with the purpose. A beach house should look like a beach house, not a chic loft.

3. The bedroom is the first thing a guest looks at. Make them inviting and comfortable. Proper bedding is key

and should include decorative pillows, a bolster, extra large shams, and a throw blanket. White or dark sheets. Use hospitality-grade linens and towels for durability. No stains, rips, or roughness. Use covers on mattresses and pillows.

4. Your furniture will experience higher traffic than in a typical house setting. Design for durability, cleanliness, and design like a stylish, darker couch and hard-surface tables that are easy to clean and don't scratch. Avoid glass tops that can shatter or complicated crystal lighting that takes a long time to clean.

5. Keep in mind the guests you are targeting. For business travelers, a desk, fast wifi, and strong coffee. For couples, fun games, plush bedding, and restaurant recommendations. For a beach house, beach chairs, kids' toys, and boogie boards.

Chapter 16:
Act Like a Hotel

As a manager and host, you are in the service business and your priority is the comfort and happiness of the guest. Be generous, understanding, and accommodating. If you have never been in a service business, people can unreasonable, irrational, and self centered; be nice anyway.

Although you're not a Ritz Carlton, you must think of yourself as one and give the guest what they need with the highest level of service. In a hotel, you can call the front desk and the concierge will answer within a few rings and "send someone up" to help you. As a remote property manager, that's not possible, but you can surprise and delight your guest in other ways.

The first 24 hours are the most important part of any stay.

First impressions last a lifetime, so the check-in must be seamless. A guest's worst nightmare is a locked door and an unreachable host. Ideally, you would meet the guest, but with multiple properties, that's not always possible or necessary. Also, most guests are overly optimistic with their arrival time and I've stood around a lot, waiting for hours. Establishing that first connection face-to-face almost always makes for a better stay and review, but you can make the check-in just as good with well-thought-out instructions and communication.

In the Airbnb app, set up your check-in instructions with pictures and descriptions of the property location, front door, and anything they need to know like parking, as well as bedroom and bathroom locations. Use a smart lock, like one from August.com, and it will sync to Airbnb and automatically send a self-generated code to the guest and stay active only for the duration of their trip. If you don't want to install a lock, get a Masterlock lockbox, like the real estate agents use.

Upon arrival, I like to leave a light on, along with a hand-written note and an inexpensive bottle of wine to accompany our Welcome Book and gift basket.

"Hey _(name)___

Welcome to _(City)___! Here's something to get the party started, on me.

Enjoy, Ryan"

In addition, all the listings have:

- A gift basket with protein bars, popcorn, and a bottle of water, bought in bulk from Amazon.
- A full-length fleece bathrobe and spa slippers.
- Polaroid camera that guests are encouraged to take a selfie with so we can attach it to our guest wall.
- The Welcome Book tailored to the space (which I will describe in the next section) with house info and personal recommendations.

- One USB charging station with multiple ports and a wireless charger.

- Amazon Firestick loaded with a Netflix account.

- Nest wifi thermostat with sensors and set on a schedule.

- Amazon Alexa with Bluetooth speaker.

- Doorbell camera.

That all may be more than you're willing to do, but maybe these reviews will sway you otherwise.

"A truly luxurious experience! This loft is lavishly outfitted and the room and bathroom had every comfort and plenty of welcome touches, from perfect pillows to a basket of snacks. An incredible value and perfect location, Ryan was an attentive and generous host!"

"This is THE place to stay in St. Louis! Both my partner and I have stayed in many Airbnbs across the US and around the world, and we've rarely felt as welcome and as comfortable in a space as Ryan's. If you're headed to the gateway to the west, look no further than this spot. It really is the coolest loft in the city."

I love reading reviews like this and creating an experience people will remember. It means a lot to me that these happy guests took the time to express their appreciation.

When you have everything ready, what better way to see how it all came together than to "sleep in your own bed". Be your own guest for a night! Sleep in the bed, try out the towels, take a shower, make breakfast in the morning. This will ensure everything is comfortable, working, and ready for your first guests.

Chapter 17:
<u>The Welcome Book</u>

Guests use Airbnb to live like a local. They want to know the best place for a hotdog while in DC and the best beach to hit in San Diego. They want the real deal, the inside scoop. So I created a Welcome Book, personal to each space. This is where we hosts can shine, as it's our version of a concierge. But instead of pushing a guest to a spot where we get a kickback, we give guests our untrained recommendations, unbound to any partnership or corporate structure. We are free with our advice, unlike a hotel.

The guests gets exactly what they want; an authentic experience.

I designed the book using Canva (free graphic design software) to make it professional. Then we brought it to Fedex to have it lamented and spiral bound to hold up against wear and tear.

It's divided into three sections: story and house, important information, and personal recommendations.

For story and house, I include my contact information and the fact that I manage the space for the owners. I describe the house with some background information like when it was built, who lived there, and any special features.

For important information, I include WiFi, TV instructions, lighting operations, how to lock the doors, and the house rules (like the smoking policy and noise levels).

For recommendations, I share points of interest and activities close by, along with a two-sentence description of each. Places like a coffee shop, local restaurant favorites, grocery stores, and the nearest pharmacy. Make a recommendation with a personal touch. "I love Blackthron Pub. One time we saw a mouse run across the floor, but the pizza is so good, it's worth the trip and shielding your eyes."

For a copy of one of my own Welcome Book, go to CashPadBook.com/welcome

Along with the Welcome Book, I also include free local magazines available at any Whole Foods or grocery store. These have up-to-date events, local news, and food recommendations.

It's all about options. Guests can either ask for specifics, browse the guest book for general recommendations, or check the local materials. Whichever they prefer.

Chapter 18:
<u>House Rules</u>

Coming up with a few rules and boundaries is a good idea. You don't want them to be so strict that a guest feels like they're staying at their parents' house, but you do need enough to keep everyone on their best behavior. In plain and simple language, they should cover:

- Smoking: Strictly prohibited or allowed in certain areas? Both nicotine and marijuana? (Welcome to 2019.)

- Extra Guests: How many people are allowed in the unit at a time? How many are allowed to stay overnight?

- Noise levels: Do you have quiet hours? After 10pm during the week? 11pm on weekends?

- Shoes: Off at the front door?

- Parking: Where? This can also be shown in your check-in pictures.

- Cleaning: Dishes put away before they leave? Dishwasher running? Trash put in the dumpster? This can also be in the automatic message sent the night before check-out as a reminder.

This is a personal home, not a hotel, and it should be treated as such. With these rules in a place a guest should enjoy their time but also be respectful of the environment. As a host, you have the right to ask guests to leave if they break any of the rules.

Chapter 19:
<u>Bad Apples</u>

With Airbnb becoming more popular, you may run into more problems. No longer are guests only the adventurous community-based type. Now it's hit the mainstream and the general public may not know how to act appropriately or truly understand they are in a personal home and not a corporate hotel. Be cautious of profiles with short names and no pictures or reviews.

At the same time, keep in mind that because Airbnb is still new and 35% of bookings are from first timers, that most haven't built up their profile yet. If you have suspicions, investigate and feel them out by asking questions. What is the purpose of their stay? Short answer messages are usually another sign the guest may not be a good fit for you.

If something seems off, don't hesitate to deny a booking.

If a bad apple passes through your tests and you unfortunately have a bad experience, I'd first try to come to an agreement with the guest before getting Airbnb involved. Keep all communication on the Airbnb messaging platform. Avoid texting and phone calls, that way there are records if you need to file a claim with the Airbnb Resolution Center.

So far, in my time hosting over 100 bookings, I've had only two negative experiences. The first, a guest invited 20 people over for a big family dinner without warning. Once my neighbor alerted me to the large groups of people coming in and out, I called the guest and he left amicability without issue, so I did not leave a review nor did he. The other used the house to shoot a music video and light off smoke bombs. This time, I left a negative review after the guest refused to pay for the extra cleaning supplies we used to get the smell out.

Chapter 20:
Pricing

When deciding your nightly rate, one approach is to look at the competition and see what the market is supporting. When I did this, I was shocked at how cheap hosts were offering up their homes. However, don't be fooled by this. Airbnb will show the lowest rate available. Click a listing's calendar and you'll see a wide range of nightly rates that adjusts depending on demand and availability. Some listings show $40 if you book tomorrow but $140 if you book a few weeks out.

Initially, my pricing was a shot in the dark, a mixture of the market and what I deemed the space to be worth based on the level of service and extras. Once the bookings slowed down, I looked more closely and ran the numbers.

For my personal loft, I wanted to earn a $1,000 a month. If you divide total need by 30 (days in a month) you'll come up with your daily break-even amount, which is $33. At $33 a night with 100% occupied, I would cover the mortgage and live for free. Sweet deal.

So using Airbnb's Smart Pricing, a sophisticated algorithm, I set my minimum to $40 (about 20% over the break-even to account for vacancies) and my maximum to $120 (3x the minimum). Then I let the computer do the rest.

I found their pricing machine to be adequate. There are other services with monthly memberships or a percentage of booking (like Airgms.com and BeyondPricing.com) that claim they can get the best possible rate but I haven't used them personally. You might be able to squeeze a few dollars more, but then you have to factor in added costs and learn how to operate a new program. I prefer a much simpler and straightforward approach.

For your pricing, factor in the owners' mortgage expenses + a $500 management fee for your time and effort and you would get your fixed costs.

As an example, an owner has a $500,000 house and a $1,500 monthly payment. Add $500 for management and you end up with $2,000 fixed costs. Divide that by 30 (days in a month) to get your break-even, which is $66. So assuming 100% booking, $66 covers the owners' mortgage and your management fee. Then add 20% to make up for vacancies and you would be at a nightly rate of $80 as a minimum price. Multiple that by 3 to get your maximum, which is $240.

Play around with the numbers, as this is both a science and an art. Airbnb won't take into account your specific home like a great view, a hot tub on the roof, or being in the hip part of town.

If you're over 80% occupancy, raise your rate. If you're at 60-80%, you're in the sweet spot. Anything below 60% and you're too high.

For management fees, I'd recommend 30-40% of total bookings.

Your duties would include:

- All cleaning and turnover service
- Guest check-in/check-out and key drop
- Answering all inquiries and messages
- Emergency lock-out services
- Quick electrical or plumbing issues
- All guest correspondence, including recommendations and questions

Here's how it looks in practice:

A guest books a long weekend for 3 nights at a $150 rate, plus a $70 cleaning fee. The total payout is $520. $312 goes to the owner (60%) and $208 to you (40%). After you pay the cleaners $60 ($20 x 3 hours), you end up with $148. Multiply that by 4 other listings that weekend and over a long weekend you just made close to $600. With the outsourcing I laid out in the previous chapters, you won't be working more than a couple hours a week. Multiply that over an entire month and that's a life-changing $2,400 in your pocket!

For payout, Airbnb offers a split payout tool where you can set the percentages and it will direct deposit into both you and the owners' bank accounts. They really thought of everything.

Chapter 21:
<u>Ranking</u>

There are currently 4 million listings on Airbnb. With it getting more popular by the day, it's becoming more challenging to stand out. Airbnb doesn't disclose how their ranking system works and why listings appear in the order in which they do, but like any Internet business, you want to be appear on the first page because your bookings depend on it.

Publicly, Airbnb has said it rewards its host that provide exceptional service.

When I had the problem with the house party guest, my bookings slowed down for over a month.

Your appeal, price, reviews, verification, and responsiveness are all factored into the ranking. Beyond that, I've noticed a domino effect with regard to bookings; once I get a few in a row, they start pouring in. I've also heard rumors that being "favorited" or "wish listed" will help you show up higher as well. The treehouse in Atlanta (#2 most popular) only accepts bookings from guests who have it wish listed, probably for that very reason.

https://expandedramblings.com/index.php/Airbnb-statistics/

Chapter 22:
<u>Reviews</u>

This all hinges on trust. Guest like to see what others are saying before they make a decision. Hosts live and die by their reviews, so do everything you can to keep your guests happy, raving fans. One negative review could be a death blow, especially in the beginning when every single one counts. With new listings I suggest pricing lower, so that you book up faster and earn more reviews.

The best way to ensure a review is to leave one first. The guests will get an email notifying them you did with the text blocked out. I found this to be a great reminder and motivator, since we're curious what people say about us.

I write all my reviews personally and thoughtfully. I take into account any conversation or message we exchange, the check-in/check-out, the condition they left the house in, if they followed the house rules, and if I would recommend them to future hosts.

Having top-notch reviews will help you climb the listing ladder in your city. You'll appear higher in the search results. And more reviews equals more bookings. I've found being communicative is the best way to earn a high rating. If a guest has a question or a problem, you should answer in a timely manner. Another way is to be helpful and make sure the space is accurate to the pictures, clean, and functional.

Airbnb shows the data the guests left for six categories:

- Accuracy: Do the pictures match? Did you overpromise?

- Communication: Were you responsive and reachable during their stay?

- Cleanliness: Was it hotel-standard clean?

- Location: Are you in a safe and convenient area?

- Check-in: Was it easy to locate and enter?

- Value: Did they get what they paid for?

With this specific information, you can improve their experience and pinpoint areas for improvement. For example, I solicited feedback when I noticed my cleaning rating was consistently low and then discussed it with my cleaner.

Bottom line: To earn a great review, ensure your listing is spotless, that everything works, and you care about your guest. Communication: Were you there for them?

Chapter 23:
<u>Superhost</u>

A Superhost means you provide exceptional service and guests love you. Determined by a few factors, it's the crown jewel of Airbnb and you must earn it as fast as you can.

In order to do so, every three months you must have:

- Completed at least 10 trips

- Maintained a 50% review rate or higher

- Maintained a 90% response rate or higher

- Zero cancellations, with exceptions made for those that fall under an extenuating policy

- Maintain a 4.8 overall rating

The benefits of becoming one are:

- A badge on all your listings

- Travel coupons
- Priority support from Airbnb

Beyond that, it gives you extra credibility and a seal of approval.

Chapter 24:
Best Practices

Respond to every message! Legend has it Airbnb will reward those that do by bumping you up in the algorithm. Download the app so you can be reachable and responsive from your phone. As a general rule, during times you're awake, get back to a guest within the hour. They can see your response rate and response time on the listing page and it may affect their decision to book. Be prompt, concise, and friendly.

Never cancel a booking. Avoid it all costs. Not only will this result in the loss of Superhost status, it will show up on your reviews. Traveling is supposed to be relaxing and the guest may already be on edge, taking a risk by staying in a stranger's home. Airbnb wants reliable hosts and a cancellation, which leads to the guest trying to scramble to find something else, is something they don't take kindly to.

The guest is always right. When it comes to fixable problems, take care of them right away. When a guest clogged the toilet, I sent my maintenance guy over within the hour. When a guest complained about cleanliness, I refunded their cleaning fee. When a guest complained about dust, I went out to home depot and bought a dehumidifier for them.

Allow early check-in or check-out if possible. This all comes down to being accommodating to your guests.

Chapter 25:
<u>Next Step</u>

I treat this as a side business personally, but it can be a full-time gig if you wish. With all the opportunity, you can be like my friend in NYC managing 30+ listings making a million or you can manage only a hand full and earn $50k. Seventy-five percent of hosts are earning less than $10,000 a year. Follow the steps in the book and you can be a Superhost earning much more than that.

If you enjoy hosting, dislike your job, and see a need in your city, then by all means go all in. The sky is the limit.

When I first started hosting, I just wanted to cover my mortgage so I could invest that money into my gym. After a year, I wanted to help others do it, because I learned how to be a great host and it turned out to be fairly simple and rewarding.

I personally believe you can manage up to eight locations as a one-person business. The more listings you have, the harder it becomes to manage. You need to have teams, multiple cleaners, and software. There is an opportunity cost here, and it will take more of your time as you juggle more plates.

For me, a few is plenty right now.

There is always this desire for more, especially in America. How big and how many are the first two questions that come to mind. We become market driven rather than driving the market.

Go deep with your guests. Meet their needs, be generous, and be proud of the work you do. Change them for the better in creating an experience they'll never forget. To me, that's considered a thriving short-term rental business.

Send me an email at Ryan@CashPadBook.com when you have your first space. I want to read your story and hear all about your own journey. To hear about how you took the information and put it to use is the ultimate joy for me.

If you need additional help or resources, or if you still have questions, you can apply for private coaching, as I take on a few clients to work with more directly. You can also sign up for an in-depth course covering the exact templates and documents I use in my own business. Go to CashPadBook.com for more information.

I urge you not delay on this. I've never seen an opportunity so big staring at all of us right in the face. It's ripe for the picking, so please take advantage and move quickly. If you're reading this, you can already see what's happening and it won't always be this way. This window is slowly closing. Good luck and thanks for reading!

- Ryan

Success Stories

Jeremy - St. Louis, MO

Jeremy quit his full time job to pursue short-term rental management. Before Airbnb, he managed his own a duplex for a couple years doing long-term rentals. It wasn't until he and his wife went on vacation for 10 days and decided to list their space on the site that they decided to make the switch. That first stay paid for a big chunk of their trip, so it caught their attention. They tripled their income, bringing in $2,000 a month after expenses, spending only four hours a week managing it.

Now they manage their own space plus a friend's for a percentage. In the next year, they plan to add four to six more through a relationship with another property management company. "I only see demand increasing from here."

Paul - Chicago, IL

Paul owns a construction company and has been managing Airbnbs since 2015. After hearing about it through an employee, he decided to list his own space first. How he manages six others. Last year his property brought in $85,000 and $5,500 through managing the others. "My business has grown every year. I keep raising prices and booking out 4+ months and 99% of guests are super friendly."

Bonus Chapter: How to Write a Book

The idea for a book sparked after people became interested in what I was doing with hosting. They knew I loved it, that I was making money, and that I would have stories of great guests who left chocolates and gushing reviews.

I can help others do what I did, I thought. I sat down and scribbled out the title of chapters that came off the top of my head on a yellow legal pad. Reviews, listings, pictures.

Then I wrote. I fired up Pages on my Mac and started with the intro, my story, and then the nitty gritty about how I do it. I was surprised how it all came pouring out of me since this was my first time writing a book. I suggest writing what you know best so it feels painless. I was essentially writing the book already in the back of my head during every guest stay. When I sat down to do it, I was reciting my experience and memories.

For my process, I first wrote a skeleton of the entire book, filling in bits for every chapter that included paragraphs, words, or phrases. I put down everything that came to mind.

Some days were strictly about writing, others were editing, and few were reading. I wrote at the house, library, and coffee shop.

On writing days, my goal was to achieve 1,000 words a day or two hours of concentrated effort, whichever came first. I did my best to never miss a day and if I did, I did my double best to not miss two in a row. An object in motion stays in motion. The restart would feel burdensome and discourage me. So little by little I went forward, leaving some in the tank so I didn't burn myself out. Sometimes I'd even cut myself off mid sentence as a tease, so that I could come back the next day chomping at the bit.

I set a hard deadline for a month to have it written, edited, designed, and formatted. I haven't decided if this will only be an ebook or if I want to make a hardcover, as well.

Eventually, I found an editor and formatter on Fiverr.com after about a few hours of reading reviews and sifting through samples of their work.

Right as I was about to finish this book, I got incredibly sick with the flu and it sold me even more on the value of daily writing. The seven days I spend on my deathbed set me back. Being bored and bedridden, thinking about my book (which was pretty much all I could do) made my heart hurt even more. Write every day. This way you can drop into your zone and let the words flow out. I've heard of authors booking month-long vacations just so they can write uninterrupted.

I hope this helps. You don't have to do it my way, but if you do want to write a book, you can shoulder that burden with solid practice. It takes a lot fortitude and discipline to continue on in our modern distracted world that tries so hard to pull you in a thousand different directions. Keep going because it's worth it. Even if no one reads it, at least you can say you did it and that satisfaction alone can beat any review.

Resources

To start listing, www.Airbnb.com/r/rhansen369

For more information, CashPadBook.com

For questions or comments, Ryan@CashPadBook.com

For networking, Meetup.com

For a proposal, CashPadBook.com/proposal

For cleaning, Care.com

For market research, Airdna.com

For maintenance, TaskRabbit.com

For messages, SuperHostTools.com

For an assistant, ZenDesk.com or VirtualStaffFinder.com

For pictures, Homejab.com

For design, CashPadBook.com/design

For smartlock, August.com

For welcome book, CashPadBook.com/welcome

For pricing, Airgms.com or BeyondPricing.com

For editing and formating, Fiverr.com

www.ingramcontent.com/pod-product-compliance
Lightning Source LLC
Chambersburg PA
CBHW020606220526
45463CB00006B/2479